To Graham

500 of the Most Witty, Acerbic and Erudite Things Ever Said About Politics

Best wishes

Iain Dale

Compiled by
Iain Dale

HARRIMAN HOUSE LTD
3A Penns Road
Petersfield
Hampshire
GU32 2EW
GREAT BRITAIN

Tel: +44 (0)1730 233870
Fax: +44 (0)1730 233880
Email: enquiries@harriman-house.com
Website: www.harriman-house.com

First published in Great Britain in 2007
Copyright © Harriman House Ltd

The right of Iain Dale to be identified as Author has been asserted in accordance
with the Copyright, Design and Patents Act 1988

ISBN: 1-9056-4131-1
ISBN 13: 978-19056413-14

British Library Cataloguing in Publication Data
A CIP catalogue record for this book can be obtained from the British Library.

Printed and bound in Great Britain by The Bath Press, CPI Group

Illustrations courtesy of Hoby, www.hobycartoons.com

Preface

When Harriman House asked me to compile this book I thought long and hard about the best way to do it. I didn't want just to list 500 random quotes which either amused, impressed or inspired me. In the end I decided to look at it from the viewpoint of someone who was interested in politics, but until now hadn't really done anything about it. So it's aimed at, not to put too fine a point on it, political virgins. It takes you through the whole political process, from defining what politics is, through to standing for election, making speeches, holding power, being involved in scandal and finally, bowing out.

Politics continues to fascinate. Political parties may, on the surface, appear very similar in outlook, approach and policies, but underneath they are as tribal as they ever were. Politicians are caught in a quandary. On the one hand people say "why can't you just agree with each other?" but on the other hand they demand a real choice. After all, if you can't tell the difference why on earth would you bother to get out of bed on a wet Thursday morning to go and vote?

At the beginning of the twenty-first century the quotes in this book illustrate the sharp divide that exists between the left and right of the political spectrum. It's not quite like Ted Hunt once said: "The Conservatives conserve what you have got, the Liberals are liberal with it and Labour gives it all away" – but it's not far off.

The overwhelming theme of this book is that politics can be fun and humorous. Some of the humour is intentional but much is not. Take a parliamentary question from Dame Irene Ward MP during the war: "Is my right honourable friend saying that Wrens' skirts must be held up until all sailors have been satisfied?" You can't really follow that, can you?

Ronald Reagan memorably said: "Politics is not a bad profession. If you succeed, there are many rewards; if you disgrace yourself, you can always write a book." I can't actually remember disgracing myself, but here's the book anyway!

Iain Dale

Tunbridge Wells, April 2007

About the author

Iain Dale is Britain's leading political blogger. He is a political commentator for the BBC and Sky and presents a daily political chat show on the internet TV station 18DoughtyStreet.com. He has fortnightly columns in the *Daily Telegraph* and the *Eastern Daily Press*. Iain is a former Conservative Party candidate and was Chief of Staff to David Davis during the Conservative Party leadership contest. He is the author and editor of more than a dozen books including *Margaret Thatcher: A Tribute in Words & Pictures, Memories of the Falklands* and *The Tony Blair New New Labour Joke book*.

Iain's blog can be read at:

http://iaindale.blogspot.com

First principles

A guide to politics

Politics is the art of acquiring, holding, and wielding power.

Indira Gandhi

Politics is the art of the possible.

R. A. Butler

Politics is the art of choosing between the disastrous and the unpalatable.

J. K. Galbraith

All politics is local.

Tip O'Neill

Politics is trying to get into office.

William McMahon

Politics is a marathon, not a sprint.

Ken Livingstone

Nothing in politics is ever as good or as bad as it first appears.

Edward Boyle

You never reach the Promised Land. You can march towards it.

James Callaghan

The art of politics

The art of politics consists in knowing precisely when it is necessary to hit an opponent slightly below the belt.

Konrad Adenauer

A politician who enters public life may as well face the fact that the best way of not being found out is not to do anything which, if found out, will cause his ruin.

Lord Hailsham

Politics is not a bad profession. If you succeed, there are many rewards; if you disgrace yourself, you can always write a book.

Ronald Reagan

In politics, what begins in fear, usually ends in folly.

Samuel Taylor Coleridge

The only thing you can be certain about in politics is that you can't be certain about anything.

Tony Banks

Never believe anything in politics until it has been officially denied.

Otto von Bismarck

Responsibility is a value shared. If it doesn't apply to everyone it ends up applying to no one.

Tony Blair

Being a politician

Politicians are like children, you can't give them what they want, it only encourages them.

Frank Weasel, Jim Hacker's Special Adviser

The politician's prayer is: May my words be ever soft and low, for I may have to eat them.

Norman Lamont

A politician is a person who approaches every subject with an open mouth.

Adlai Stevenson

They say a man should be judged by his enemies. I am very proud of mine.

Michael Heseltine

A politician was a person with whose politics you did not agree. When you did agree, he was a statesman.

David Lloyd George

A statesman is a politician who places himself at the service of the nation. A politician is a statesman who places the nation at his service.

Georges Pompidou

We are not in politics to ignore people's worries, we are in politics to deal with them.

Margaret Thatcher

Politicians are just as human as everyone else.

David Blunkett

Politicians are like nappies; they both need changing regularly and for the same reason.

Anonymous

Political timing

In politics there is no use in looking beyond the next fortnight.

Joseph Chamberlain

A week is a long time in politics.

Harold Wilson

I would not say that the future is necessarily less predictable than the past. I think the past was not predictable when it started.

Donald Rumsfeld

Clearly the future is still to come.

Peter Brooke

I have found the future rather difficult to predict before it happens.

Roy Jenkins

At the end of the day, isn't it time we called it a day?

John Morris

The future is not what it used to be.

Malcolm Rifkind

So you want to be a politician?

Considering a political career?

I got fed up with all the sex and sleaze and backhanders of rock and roll so I went into politics.

Tony Blair

Politicians are exiles from the normal, private world.

John Grigg

Teaching is a good preparation for politics because you have to reply to questions when you don't know the answer.

Keith Best

Being an MP feeds your vanity and starves your self respect.

Matthew Parris

Wise advice

In politics you get what you deserve rather than what you want.

Cecil Parkinson

Don't be afraid to take a big step. You can't cross a chasm in two small jumps.

David Lloyd George

You have to be in the arena to make a difference.

Richard Nixon

You can't adopt politics as a profession, and remain honest.

Louis McHenry Howe

You may fool all the people some of the time; you can even fool some of the people all of the time; but you can't fool all the people all the time.

Abraham Lincoln

One golden rule for people who want to get on in politics is to keep their traps shut in August.

W. F. Deedes

The only thing we
have to
fear is
fear itself.
*Franklin D.
Roosevelt*

When it is not necessary to change, it is necessary not to change.

Viscount Falkland

Don't expect any thanks

If politicians lived on praise and thanks they'd be forced into some other line of business.

Edward Heath

Whenever I am told that politicians are among the lowest form of human life, I thank God I am not an estate agent.

Jack Straw

Loyalty

Loyalty is a fine quality, but in excess it fills political graveyards.

Neil Kinnock

Do you know what loyalty means in a Cabinet Minister? It means his fear of losing his job is only slightly greater than his hope of pinching mine.

Jim Hacker

Disloyalty is the secret weapon of the Tory Party.

Julian Critchley

Skills you need

Political skill is the ability to foretell what is going to happen...and to have the ability afterwards to explain why it did not happen.

Winston Churchill

If you want to succeed in politics, you must keep your conscience well under control.

David Lloyd George

Great expectations

There is now a recognition that we cannot expect people to vote for us just on our say so.

Peter Kilfoyle

As a politician, you only meet two types of people; People with problems, and people who are right.

Gyles Brandreth

Having fun

Politics should be fun.

Lord Hailsham

Safe is spelled D.U.L.L. Politics has got to be a fun activity.

Alan Clark

Never whinge

You will find in politics that you are much exposed to the attribution of false motive. Never complain and never explain.

Stanley Baldwin

Being wrong is one of the privileges of public life, and indeed it is widely practised.

Tony Benn

Shrinking violets

A thick skin is a gift from God.

Konrad Adenauer

The most successful politician is he who says what everybody is thinking most often and in the loudest voice.

Theodore Roosevelt

Promises promises

Politicians are the same all over. They promise to build bridges, even where there are no rivers.

Nikita Khruschev

The worst thing a politician can do is over-promise and then under-deliver.

Iain Dale

Not that I'm one to gossip

The first law of political indiscretion; always have a drink before you leak.

Jim Hacker

Your flexible friend

Protection is not a principle, but an expedient.

Benjamin Disraeli

Finality is not the language of politics.

Benjamin Disraeli

Since a politician never believes what he says, he is quite surprised to be taken at his word.

Charles de Gaulle

Problems & solutions

You are either part of the solution or you are part of the problem.

Eldridge Cleaver

Politicians are entitled to change their minds. But when they adjust their principles some explanation is necessary.

Roy Hattersley

Self-awareness

It is never wise to try to appear to be more clever than you are. It is sometimes wise to appear slightly less so.

William Whitelaw

I'm vulgar, I'm a populist. But isn't that what the mayor should be?

Jeffrey Archer, on his London mayoral bid

Image

It's expensive to be in politics. One has to be mobile, one has to be well groomed, and one has to entertain.

Margaret Thatcher

I'm an optimist. But I'm an optimist who takes my raincoat.

Harold Wilson

Politicians are the easiest people to con because they want to believe in appearances.

Alistair McAlpine

Was I ever one of us?

Kenneth Baker

Gaffe-prone?

No man ever became great or good except through many and great mistakes.

William Ewart Gladstone

Every politician is allowed the occasional gaffe, if only to remind the public that they are still human.

Peter Mandelson

First law on holes: When you are in one, stop digging.

Denis Healey

Face up to your negatives

I have never found my educational background a problem with ordinary voters. I have only ever found it a problem with middle-class journalists.

Tony Blair

Normally when I'm asked on holiday and I say what I do, I say I'm a traffic warden. That makes me much more popular.

Stephen Pound

Getting elected

Why bother?

There's a lot of bleeding idiots in t'country and they deserve some representation.

Bill Stones

Are you depressed, unhappy, suicidal? Then think what it's like for me as a Conservative candidate!

Election address of Manchester Conservative Candidate, John Kelly in 1995

The public will get the kind of public men it deserves.

Lord Hailsham

You won the elections, but I won the count.

Anastazio Somoza

The point of an election

An election is like a violent love affair.

Chips Channon

To elect and to reject is the prerogative of a free people.

Thomas Paine

First rule of politics: You can't win unless you're on the ballot. Second rule: If you run, you may lose. And, if you tie, you do not win.

Donald Rumsfeld

General elections

We had lost the art of communication – but not, alas, the gift of speech.

Gordon Brown on Labour's 1983 election campaign

Sounding like a mixture of Victor Meldrew and Colonel Blimp does not constitute a coherent policy or a basis for political appeal.

Alan Duncan

What the electorate gives, the electorate can take away.

Tony Blair

If voting changed anything, they'd abolish it.

Ken Livingstone

Harold Wilson is going around the country stirring up apathy.

William Whitelaw

The moral high ground

I will not take the low road to the highest office in the land. I want the presidency in the best way, not the worst way.

John McCain

Better we lose the election than mislead the people.

Adlai Stevenson

The desire to win is born in most of us. The will to win is a matter of training. The manner of winning is a matter of honour.

Denis Thatcher

Advice for the voter

Vote for the man who promises least – he'll be the least disappointing.

Bernard Baruch

When moral principles, rather than persons, are candidates for power, to vote is to perform a moral duty, and not to vote is a neglect of duty.

Thomas Paine

Ambition

When I was five I wanted to be prime minister, now I would rather poke my eyes out with a fork.

Oona King

Any American who is prepared to run for President should automatically, by definition, be disqualified from ever doing so.

Gore Vidal

I have climbed to the top of the greasy pole.

Benjamin Disraeli

The office of the Prime Minister is what its holder chooses and is able to make of it.

Herbert Asquith

Leadership

I intend to march my troops towards the sound of gunfire.

Jo Grimond

The art of leadership is saying no, not yes. It is very easy to say yes.

Tony Blair

In the end leaders are leaders. They get the credit and they get the blame.

Michael Heseltine

The successful leader does not talk down to people. He lifts them up.

Richard Nixon

Leadership is not about nice. It's about being right and being strong.

Paul Keating

It's the people's will, I am their leader, I must follow them.

Jim Hacker

Do not follow where the path may lead. Go instead where there is no path and leave a trail.

Anonymous

Society's demands for moral authority and character increase as the importance of the position increases.

John Adams

A man who wants to act virtuously in every way necessarily comes to grief among so many who are not virtuous.

Niccolo Machiavelli

Democracy

Definitions

Democracy is being allowed to vote for the candidate you dislike least.

Robert Byrne

I don't know exactly what democracy is. But we need more of it.

Anonymous Chinese Student, during protests in Tianamen Square, Beijing

Democracy is a pathetic belief in the collective wisdom of individual ignorance.

H. L. Mencken

Democracy means government by discussion, but it is only effective if you can stop people talking.

Clement Attlee

In democracy everyone has the right to be represented, even the jerks.

Chris Patten

The alternative

Democracy substitutes election by the incompetent many for appointment by the corrupt few.

George Bernard Shaw

It has been said that democracy is the worst form of government except all the others that have been tried.

Winston Churchill

Corruption is nature's way of restoring our faith in democracy.

Peter Ustinov

The experience of democracy is like the experience of life itself – always changing, infinite in its variety, sometimes turbulent and all the more valuable for having been tested by adversity.

Jimmy Carter

Democracy forever teases us with the contrast between its ideals and its realities, between its heroic possibilities and its sorry achievements.

Agnes Repplier

If liberty and equality, as is thought by some, are chiefly to be found in democracy, they will be best attained when all persons alike share in the government to the utmost.

Aristotle

Democracy is the recurrent suspicion that more than half of the people are right more than half of the time.

E. B. White

As long as the differences and diversities of mankind exist, democracy must allow for compromise, for accommodation, and for the recognition of differences.

Eugene McCarthy

In 1929 the wise, far-seeing electors of my native Hereford sent me to Westminster and, two years later, the lousy bastards kicked me out.

Frank Owen

Democracy does not guarantee equality of conditions – it only guarantees equality of opportunity.

Irving Kristol

Speech making, oratory & spin

Rules

There are three golden rules for Parliamentary speakers: Stand up, speak up and shut up.

James Lowther

Better keep your mouth shut and be thought a fool than open it and remove all doubt.

Denis Thatcher

A good speech may not always be remembered but a bad speech is never forgotten – or forgiven.

Bernard Weatherill

On your feet

A speech is like a love affair. Any fool can start it, but to end it requires considerable skill.

Lord Mancroft

Making a speech on economics is a bit like pissing down your leg. It seems hot to you but never to anyone else.

Lyndon Johnson

If the word 'No' was removed from the English language, Ian Paisley would be speechless.

John Hume

Eloquence & oratory

We will never forget them, nor the last time we saw them this morning, as they prepared for the journey and waved goodbye and 'slipped the surly bonds of earth' to 'touch the face of God'.

Ronald Reagan on the loss of the space shuttle Challenger

You cannot help the poor by destroying the rich. You cannot lift the wage earner by pulling down the wage payer.

Abraham Lincoln

Let us never negotiate out of fear. But let us never fear to negotiate.

John F. Kennedy

Ask not what your country can do for you. Ask what you can do for your country.

John F. Kennedy

The media

You know Bernard, I sometimes think our Minister doesn't believe that he exists unless he is reading about himself in the paper.

Sir Humphrey Appleby

Politicians who complain about the media are like ships' captains who complain about the sea.

Enoch Powell

Unreconstructed wankers.

Tony Blair's description of the Scottish media

The press is a tiger, and whether you like it or not in politics, you are put astride it but it is a pretty fearsome beast.

Tony Blair

Those who live by the media die by it more often than not. My first witness on that point is Peter Mandelson.

David Mellor

Interviewing politicians can be like nailing custard to the wall.

John Humphrys

A soundbite never buttered a parsnip.

John Major

Spin

I would not know a focus group if I met one. I am unspun.

Frank Dobson

The wages of spin are disrepute and decay.

Sir Bernard Ingham

We should always tell the press freely and frankly anything they could easily find out any other way.

Sir Humphrey Appleby

If I rescued a child from drowning the press would headline the story 'Benn grabs child'.

Tony Benn

I do not wear a bleeper. I can't speak in soundbites. I refuse to repeat slogans. I hate focus groups. I absolutely hate image consultants.

Kenneth Clarke

Parliament

Parliament is nothing less than a big meeting of more or less idle people.

Walter Bagehot

Sire, I have neither eyes to see nor tongue to speak in this place, but as this House is pleased to direct me, whose servant I am here; and I humbly beg Your Majesty's pardon that I cannot give any other answer than this to what Your Majesty is pleased to demand of me.

Speaker William Lenthall

When Gentlemen cease to be returned to Parliament this Empire will perish.

Benjamin Disraeli

The greatest opportunity that can be offered to an Englishman – a seat in the House of Commons.

Benjamin Disraeli

Commons & Lords

The House of Commons is absolute. It is the State. *L'etat c'est moi.*

Benjamin Disraeli

Anybody who enjoys being in the House of Commons probably needs psychiatric help.

Ken Livingstone

There is nothing more popular in the House of Commons than to blame yourself. 'I have killed my mother. I will never do it again,' is certain to raise a cheer.

Margot Asquith

At the House of Commons sword fighting is strictly taboo. Back-stabbing, on the other hand, is quite a different matter.

Gyles Brandreth

To anyone who has politics in his blood, this place is like a pub to a drunkard.

David Lloyd George on the House of Commons

The greatest test of courage I can conceive is to speak the truth in the House of Commons.

William Hazlitt

The House of Lords is like a glass of champagne that has stood for five days.

Clement Attlee

Opposition

The duty of an Opposition is very simple: To oppose everything and propose nothing.

Lord Derby

No government can be long secure without a formidable opposition.

Benjamin Disraeli

Opposition is four or five years' humiliation in which there is no escape from the indignity of no longer controlling events.

Roy Hattersley

In Parliament it should not only be the duty but the pleasure of the Opposition to oppose whenever they reasonably can.

Iain Macleod

PMQs

This grammar school boy is not going to take any lessons from a public school boy on children from less privileged backgrounds.

Michael Howard

I am happy to debate the past with the Prime Minister...I have a big dossier on his past, and I did not even have to sex it up.

Michael Howard

In a carbon conscious world, we got a fossil fuel chancellor.

David Cameron on Gordon Brown

Party discipline

Every dog is allowed one bite, but a different view is taken of a dog that goes on biting all the time. He may not get his licence returned when it falls due.

Harold Wilson, speaking to a group of rebellious Labour backbenchers

Tell your kids to get their scooters off my lawn.

Ken Clarke to Tory Party chairman Brian
Mawhinney

The whips' duty is to make a House, keep a House and cheer the Minister.

George Canning

Damn your principles! Stick to your Party.

Benjamin Disraeli

To those waiting with baited breath for that favourite media catchphrase, the U Turn, I have only one thing to say. You turn if you want to. The Lady's not for turning.

Margaret Thatcher

A little rebellion now and then is a good thing.

Thomas Jefferson

Better to have him inside the tent pissing out than outside the tent pissing in.

Lyndon Johnson on J. Edgar Hoover

Power

Being in power is like being a lady – if you have to tell people you are, you aren't.

Margaret Thatcher

Asking politicians to vote themselves out of power is like asking rabbits not to multiply, it ain't natural.

Bob Beckel

Power is the great aphrodisiac.

Henry Kissinger

What power have you got? Where did you get it from? In whose interests do you exercise it? To whom are you accountable? How do we get rid of you?

Tony Benn

Abuse of power

The greater the power, the more dangerous the abuse.

Edmund Burke

Unlimited power is apt to corrupt the minds of those who possess it; and this I know, my Lords, that where law ends, tyranny begins.

William Pitt, in the House of Lords attacking the expulsion of John Wilkes from the House of Commons

My opinion is, that power should always be distrusted, in whatever hands it is placed.

William Jones

Bernard, if the right people don't have power do you know what happens? The wrong people get it. Politicians, councillors, ordinary voters.

Sir Humphrey Appleby

Unlimited power is apt to corrupt the minds of those who possess it.

William Pitt

Power tends to corrupt and absolute power corrupts absolutely.

Lord Acton

Government

What Government is

Government of the people, by the people, for the people.

Abraham Lincoln

I look upon Parliamentary Government as the noblest government in the world.

Benjamin Disraeli

Government is a contrivance of human wisdom to provide for human wants.

Edmund Burke

Government, like dress, is the badge of lost innocence.

Thomas Paine

Government, even in its best state, is but a necessary evil; in its worst state, an intolerable one.

Thomas Paine

I have always believed that a government had a limited capacity to do good and a virtually infinite capacity to do harm.

Neil Hamilton

The first basis of government is justice, not fear.

Woodrow Wilson

If the Government is big enough to give you everything you want, it is big enough to take away everything you have.

Gerald Ford

What Government isn't

An ideal form of government is democracy tempered with assassination.

Voltaire

Dirty tricks are part and parcel of effective government.

Alan Clark

Of course the government should do what is right, but not if it effects marginal constituencies.

Frank Weasel, Jim Hacker's Special Adviser

Impressions of Government

The most terrifying words in the English language are 'I'm from the government and I'm here to help'.

Ronald Reagan

The most vital issue in British politics today is whether we really exist to serve the state or whether the state exists to serve us.

Brian Walden

No man is good enough to govern another man without the other's consent.

Abraham Lincoln

Governments are far more stupid than their people.

Dwight D. Eisenhower

I don't make jokes. I just watch the government and report the facts.

Will Rogers

You campaign in poetry. You govern in prose.

Mario Cuomo

All government is founded on compromise and banter.

Edmund Burke

Spending your money

Of all the vulgar acts of government, that of solving every difficulty that might arise by thrusting the hand into the public purse is the most illusory and contemptible.

Sir Robert Peel

A government that robs Peter to pay Paul can always depend on the support of Paul.

George Bernard Shaw

I have more government than I want, more government than I need, more government than I can afford.

John Redwood

The taxpayer – that's someone who works for the government but doesn't have to take the civil service examination.

Ronald Reagan

Inner workings

The cabinet does not propose, it decides.

Clement Attlee

The home secretary of the day should not simply be running on the bandwagon of some particular media campaign.

Charles Clarke

If the policy isn't hurting, it isn't working.

John Major

England does not love coalitions.

Benjamin Disraeli

A committee is a group of people who individually can do nothing but together can decide that nothing can be done.

Fred Allen

We're all f****ed. I'm f****ed. You're f****ed. The whole department's f****ed. It's been the biggest cock-up ever and we're all completely f****ed.

Sir Richard Mottram, former Permanent Secretary at the Department for Transport, Local Government and the Regions

Style of Government

Consultation is a good thing when people agree with you and a waste of time when people don't agree with you.

Ken Livingstone

We give the impression of being in office but not in power.

Norman Lamont

The army will hear nothing of politics from me and in return I expect to hear nothing of politics from the army.

Herbert Asquith

Good Government

Good government could never be a substitute for government by the people themselves.

Sir Henry Campbell-Bannerman

The ideal Government minister may well be someone who has no itch to run other people's lives.

Edward Grey

If any man asks me what a free government is, I answer that for any practical purposes, it is what the people think it so.

Edmund Burke

The model of a modern Prime Minister would be a kind of grotesque composite freak – someone with the dedication to duty of a Peel, the physical energy of a Gladstone, the detachment of a Salisbury, the brains of an Asquith, the balls of a Lloyd George, the world-power of a Churchill, the administrative gifts of an Attlee, the style of a Macmillan, the managerialism of a Heath and the sleep requirements of a Thatcher. Human beings do not come like that.

Peter Hennessy

Bad Government

Giving money and power to government is like giving whisky and car keys to teenage boys.

P. J. O'Rourke

I work for a government I despise, for ends I think criminal.

John Maynard Keynes

The ship of state, Bernard, is the only ship that leaks from the top.

Sir Humphrey Appleby

Diplomacy

An ambassador is an honest man sent abroad to lie for his country.

Sir Henry Wotton

A diplomat is somebody who can tell you to go to hell and leave you looking forward to the trip.

Alex Salmond

There cannot be a crisis next week. My schedule is already full.

Henry Kissinger

Yes Minister

The British civil service is a beautifully designed and effective braking system.

Shirley Williams

Britain has invented a new missile. It's called the civil service – it doesn't work and it can't be fired.

Sir Walter Walker

The three articles of Civil Service faith: it takes longer to do things quickly, it's more expensive to do them cheaply and it's more democratic to do them in secret.

Jim Hacker

Sir Humphrey: If there had been investigations which there haven't or not necessarily or I am not at liberty to say whether there have, there would have been a project team which had it existed on which I cannot comment which would now have disbanded if it had existed and the members returned to their original departments if indeed there had been any such members.

Jim Hacker: Or not as the case may be.

Sir Humphrey: Bernard, the Official Secrets Act is not to protect secrets it is to protect officials.

Sir Humphrey Appleby

Minister, I am neither pro nor anti anything. I am merely a humble vessel into which Ministers pour the fruits of their deliberations.

Jim Hacker

Politicians are dependant on us, a thousand press officers to publicise their little triumphs, the Official Secrets Acts to conceal their daily disasters.

Sir Arnold Robinson (Yes Minister)

No Minister

It contains a misleading impression, not a lie. It was being economical with the truth.

Sir Robert Armstrong (during the 'Spycatcher' trial)

There are occasions when you have to say 'bollocks' to ministers.

Sir Richard Wilson

The first forty-eight hours decide whether a Minister is going to run his Office or his Office is going to run him.

Leon Henderson

Party politics

What is a political party?

Party is organised opinion.

Benjamin Disraeli

I believe that without party, Parliamentary government is impossible.

Benjamin Disraeli

A good party man puts his party above himself and his country above his party.

Winston Churchill

Party is the madness of many, for the benefit of a few.

Jonathan Swift

Party games

Put three Zionists in a room and they will form four political parties.

Levi Eshkol

I do not belong to any organised political party: I'm a democrat.

Will Rogers

Any political party that includes the word 'democratic' in its name, isn't.

Patrick Murray

Party differences

An independent is the guy who wants to take the politics out of politics.

Winston Churchill

A radical is a man with both feet planted firmly in the air. A reactionary is a somnambulist walking backwards. A conservative is a man with two perfectly good legs who, however, has never learned to walk forward. A liberal is a man who uses his legs and his hands at the behest of his head.

Franklin D. Roosevelt

The Conservatives conserve what you have got, the Liberals are liberal with it and Labour gives it all away.

Ted Hunt

Vote Labour and you build castles in the air. Vote Conservative and you can live in them.

David Frost

Labour of love

There are some of us who will fight and fight and fight again to save the Party we love.

Hugh Gaitskell

My project will be complete when the Labour Party learns to love Peter Mandelson.

Tony Blair

Each successive Labour Government has been the most rapacious, doctrinaire and unpatriotic conspiracy to be seen this side of the Iron Curtain.

Roy Jenkins

The Labour Party is not dead. Just brain dead.

Norman Tebbit

I sometimes think the Labour Party is like a pub where the mild is running out. If someone does not do something soon, all that is left will be bitter and all that is bitter will be left.

Margaret Thatcher

The Labour Party has lost the last four elections. If they lose another, they get to keep the Liberal Party.

Clive Anderson

The only leaders Labour loves are dead ones.

Robert Harris

The Labour Party is like a stagecoach: If you rattle along at great speed everybody is too exhilarated or too seasick to cause any trouble. But if you stop everybody gets out and argues about where to go next.

Harold Wilson

Socialists make the mistake of confusing individual worth with success. They believe you cannot allow people to succeed in case those who fail feel worthless.

Kenneth Baker

New Labour are for everything but nothing: tough, tender; hot, cold; soft, hard; fast, slow; for you, for me; to give, to take; to stop, to start.

William Hague

Voting for New Labour is like helping an old lady across the road while screaming 'Get a move on!' Even the Tories, who you could once rely on to be completely heartless, are pretending to care.

Boy George

I do not often attack the Labour Party. They do it so well themselves.

Edward Heath

Conservatively speaking

To be a Conservative is to prefer the tried to the untried, the fact to mystery, the actual to the possible, the limited to the unbounded, the near to the distant, the sufficient to the super-abundant, the convenient to the perfect present, laughter to utopian bliss.

Michael Oakeshott

A Tory is someone who thinks institutions are wider than those who operate them.

Enoch Powell

A Conservative is a man who does not think anything should be done for the first time.

Frank Vanderlip

A liberal conservative is a man who thinks things ought to progress but would rather they remained as they are.

Sir James Fitzjames Stephen

What is conservatism? Is it not adherence to the old and tried, against the new and untried?

Abraham Lincoln

If you want a modern, compassionate Conservative go for the real thing: that's me. I am it. It's what I think and believe. When I'm under pressure and the *Daily Mail's* having a go at me, I'll stick to my guns because that's what I believe in.

David Cameron

Compassion is a disease for which the Conservative Party is the only cure.

Teresa Gorman

Compassion is not a bolt-on extra to Conservatism. It is at its very core.

William Hague

Of course no one likes the Conservatives. They only vote for us because they think we are right.

Peter Lilley

Insulting Tories

If capitalism depended on the intellectual quality of the Conservative Party, it would end about lunchtime tomorrow.

Tony Benn

A Conservative is a man who sits and thinks, mostly sits.

Woodrow Wilson

The Conservative Party always in time forgives those who were wrong. Indeed often, in time, they forgive those who were right.

Iain Macleod

The Conservatives are nothing else but a load of kippers – two-faced and gutless.

Eric Heffer

It seems to me a barren thing this Conservatism – an unhappy cross-breed, the mule of politics that engenders nothing.

Benjamin Disraeli

Conservatives are people who look at a tree and feel instinctively that it is more beautiful than anything they can name. But when it comes to defending that tree against a highway, they will go for the highway.

Norman Mailer

Conservatives are not necessarily stupid, but most stupid people are conservatives.

John Stuart Mill

Tories are not always wrong, but they are always wrong at the right moment.

Violet Bonham Carter

The Tories always hold the view that the state is an apparatus for the protection of the swag of the property owners...Christ drove the money changers out of the temple, but you inscribe their title deed on the alter cloth.

Aneurin Bevan

A Conservative Government is an organized hypocrisy.

Benjamin Disraeli

The Tory Party never panics, except in a crisis.

Sir John Hoskyns

Liberals

If there is any emergence of a fourth party in British politics, it is the task of the Liberal Party to strangle it at birth.

Cyril Smith on the SDP

A liberal is a conservative who's been arrested.

Tom Wolfe

If God had been a Liberal, we wouldn't have had the ten commandments – we'd have had the ten suggestions.

Malcolm Bradbury

As usual the Liberals offer a mixture of sound and original ideas. Unfortunately none of the sound ideas is original and none of the original ideas is sound.

Harold Macmillan

A man who is not a Liberal at sixteen has no heart. A man who is not a Conservative at sixty has no head.

Benjamin Disraeli

Liberal – a power worshipper without power.

George Orwell

Attacking the Liberals is a difficult business, involving all the hazards of wrestling with a greased pig at a fair, and then insulting the vicar.

Chris Patten

Isms

The function of socialism is to raise suffering to a higher level.

Norman Mailer

Capitalism is the unequal distribution of wealth. Socialism is the equal distribution of poverty.

Anonymous

Communism never sleeps, never changes its objectives. Nor must we.

Margaret Thatcher

That is what capitalism is: a system that brings wealth to the many, not just the few.

Margaret Thatcher

A faith is something you die for. A doctrine is something you kill for. There is all the difference in the world.

Tony Benn

Family values

He didn't riot. He got on his bike and looked for work and he kept looking until he found it.

Norman Tebbit on his father

Freedom

Man is born free; and everywhere he is in chains.

Jean Jacques Rousseau

It is true that liberty is precious; so precious that it must be carefully rationed.

Lenin

I would remind you that extremism in the defence of liberty is no vice! And let me remind you also that moderation in the pursuit of justice is no virtue.

Barry Goldwater

There is no tyranny so despotic as that of public opinion among a free people.

Donn Platt

Apostles of freedom are ever idolised when dead, but crucified when alive.

James Connolly

Choice is the essence of ethics. If there were no choice there would be no ethics, no good, no evil. Good and evil only have meaning in so far as man is free to choose.

Margaret Thatcher

The more the state plans the more difficult planning becomes for the individual.

Friedrich von Hayek

If someone is confronting our essential liberties, if someone is inflicting injuries and harm, by God I'll confront them!

Margaret Thatcher

The enemies of freedom do not argue; they shout and they shoot.

William Ralph Inge

There are no limits on our future if we don't put limits on our people.

Jack Kemp

Freedom is an indivisible word. If we want to enjoy it and fight for it, we must be prepared to extend it to everyone, whether they are rich or poor, whether they agree with us or not, no matter what their race or the colour of their skin.

Wendell Wilkie

If a free society cannot help the many who are poor, it cannot save the few who are rich.

John F. Kennedy

The most certain test by which we judge whether a country is really free is the amount of security enjoyed by its minorities.

Lord Acton

Free speech carries with it the evil of all foolish, unpleasant venomous things that are said but, on the whole, we would rather lump them than do away with them.

Winston Churchill

Justice & the rule of law

Whenever a separation is made between liberty and justice, neither, in my opinion, is safe.

Edmund Burke

Wherever law ends, tyranny begins.

John Locke

I know no method to secure the repeal of bad or obnoxious laws so effective as their stringent execution.

Ulysses S. Grant

There are not enough jails, not enough policemen, not enough courts to enforce a law not supported by the people.

Hubert Humphrey

Injustice anywhere is a threat to justice everywhere.

Martin Luther King

The keystone of the rule of law in England has been the independence of the judges. It is the only respect in which we make any real separation of powers.

Lord Denning

Let me make this clear; my identity is just that, mine. It is not yours, it is not the state's, it is mine and mine alone. It is up to me to decide who will be privy to information about that identity. I will not, absolutely not, be fingerprinted like a criminal in order to satisfy your obsessive control freakery. This is not negotiable…

Longrider Blog on ID cards

Opportunity

Equality of opportunity means equal opportunity to be unequal.

Iain Macleod

Let our children grow tall, and some taller than others.

Margaret Thatcher

If your only opportunity is to be equal then it is not opportunity.

Margaret Thatcher

Why am I the first Kinnock in a thousand generations to be able to get to university?

Neil Kinnock

Despotism

Let's give the terrorists a fair trial and then hang them.

Senator Gary Hart, September 2001

Bureaucracy, the rule of no one, has become the modern form of despotism.

Mary McCarthy

When you stop a dictator there are always risks, but there are great risks in not stopping a dictator. My generation learned that long ago.

Margaret Thatcher

A fanatic is one who can't change his mind and won't change the subject.

Winston Churchill

When bad men combine, the good must associate; else they will fall, one by one, an unpitied sacrifice in a contemptible struggle.

Edmund Burke

Bad laws are the worst sort of tyranny.

Edmund Burke

All that is necessary for the triumph of evil is that good men do nothing.

Edmund Burke

War & conflict

Preparation for war is the sweet guaranty for peace.

Theodore Roosevelt

The great questions of the day will not be settled by means of speeches and majority decisions...but by iron and blood.

Otto von Bismarck

Once we are agreed our only weapons will be our words, then there is nothing that cannot be said, there is nothing that cannot be achieved.

David Trimble

There's a very thin dividing line between dying for Ireland and killing for Ireland.

John Hume

War is too serious a matter to be left to military men.

Georges Clemenceau

Giving peace a chance does not mean taking a chance with peace.

George Bush Snr

Politics is war without bloodshed, while war is politics with bloodshed.

Mao Tse Tung

The wrong war in the wrong place at the wrong time against the wrong enemy.

Peter Kilfoyle on Iraq

It may be true that every necessary war must also really be a just war; but it does not absolutely follow that every just war is a necessary war.

Lord Aberdeen

My home policy: I wage war; my foreign policy: I wage war. All the time I wage war.

Georges Clemenceau

The sword is the axis of the world and its power is absolute.

Charles de Gaulle

You cannot win through negotiations what you cannot win on the battlefield.

Henry Kissinger

Economics

If you mess up the finances of the country, it's ordinary people that end up paying.

Tony Blair

A low success economy is a high tax one.

Tony Blair

Taxation without representation is tyranny.

James Otis

Blessed are the young, for they shall inherit the National Debt.

Herbert Hoover

There can be no economy where there is no efficiency.

Benjamin Disraeli

The Conservative Party has never believed that the business of the government is the government of business.

Nigel Lawson

Balancing your budget is like protecting your virtue. You have to learn when to say no.

Ronald Reagan

One man's wage increase is another man's price increase.

Harold Wilson

You've taxed too much, borrowed too much and are a roadblock to reform.

David Cameron to Gordon Brown

Billions raised, billions spent. No idea where the money has gone. With a record like that the chancellor should be running for treasurer of the Labour Party.

David Cameron on Gordon Brown

There are three kinds of lies: Lies, damned lies and statistics.

Benjamin Disraeli

It's a recession when your neighbour loses his job. It's a depression when you lose your own.

Harry Truman

Recession is when your neighbour loses his job. Depression is when you lose yours. And recovery is when Jimmy Carter loses his.

Ronald Reagan

Politically there is no record of the continuance of political freedoms when economic freedoms have died.

Sir Rhodes Boyson

Bernard, subsidy is for art, for culture. It is not to be given to what the people want.

Sir Humphrey Appleby

There are two problems in my life. The political ones are insoluble and the economic ones are incomprehensible.

Alec Douglas Home

My country right or wrong

Patriotism is your conviction that this country is superior to all other countries because you were born in it.

George Bernard Shaw

My foreign policy is to be able to take a ticket at Victoria Station and go anywhere I damn well please.

Ernest Bevin

A country of long shadows on county cricket grounds, warm beer, green suburbs, dog lovers, and old maids cycling to Holy Communion through the morning mist.

John Major

There is no point in saving the currency if we lose the country that goes with it.

John Redwood

No man attached to his country could always acquiesce in the opinions of the majority.

Sir Robert Peel

A single currency is about the politics of Europe. It is about a Federal Europe by the back door.

Margaret Thatcher

The Treaty of Rome is like an incoming tide. It flows into the estuaries and up the rivers. It cannot be held back.

Lord Denning

I would die for my country but I would never let my country die for me.

Neil Kinnock

Without Britain Europe would remain a torso.

Ludwig Erhard

Why should Scottish and Welsh nationalism be seen as a noble thing when in England it is seen as something dirty?

Kenneth Baker

Sovereignty is unlimited – unlimited and illimitable.

Ernest Barker

England has saved herself by her exertions, and will, I trust, save Europe by her example.

William Pitt the Younger

Predictions

Though I sit down now, the time will come when you will hear me.

Benjamin Disraeli

There is no question of any erosion of essential national sovereignty.

Edward Heath on entering the EEC in 1971

I don't think it will come for many years. I don't think it will come in my lifetime.

Margaret Thatcher in 1972 on the possibility of a woman PM

I have absolutely no doubt at all that we will find evidence of weapons of mass destruction programmes.

Tony Blair

I am not interested in a third party. I do not believe it has any future.

Shirley Williams in 1980

I foresee a Liberal vote so massive and the number of Liberal MPs so great that we shall hold the initiative in the new Parliament.

Liberal leader David Steel in 1980

Alastair Campbell's memoirs could be worth a lot of money. Not only does he know where the bodies are buried, he buried many of them.

Iain Dale

The 21st century will not be about the battle between capitalism and socialism but between the forces of progress and the forces of conservatism.

Tony Blair

I warn you not to be ordinary, I warn you not to be young, I warn you not to fall ill, and I warn you not to grow old.

Neil Kinnock on the prospect of a Tory election victory in 1983

Admitting you were wrong

I am humble enough to recognise that I have made mistakes, but politically astute enough to have forgotten what they are.

Michael Heseltine

I don't concede it at all that the intelligence at the time was wrong.

Tony Blair on the failure to find WMDs in Iraq

Truisms & telling it like it is/Saying something but saying nothing

It is fatal in life to be right too soon.

Enoch Powell

Reading 'riting, 'rithmetic, right and wrong.

Eric Forth on the '5 Rs'

Society needs to condemn a little more and understand a little less.

John Major

A good politician is as unthinkable as an honest burglar.

H. L. Mencken

It costs just as much to train a bad teacher as it does to train a good teacher.

Margaret Thatcher

Things don't happen because Prime Ministers are very keen on them. Neville Chamberlain was very keen on peace.

Sir Humphrey Appleby

All men are born equal, but quite a few eventually get over it.

Lord Mancroft

Because you can't help everybody, it doesn't mean you can't help somebody.

Douglas Hurd

They're not coming here for the funeral, they're coming here for the politics. This is a working funeral.

Jim Hacker

In the last Parliament, the House of Commons had more MPs called John than all the women MPs put together.

Tessa Jowell

There is nothing wrong with this country which a good election can't fix.

Richard Nixon

It has always been desirable to tell the truth, but seldom if ever necessary to tell the whole truth.

Arthur Balfour

One man's priority is another man's extravagance.

Edwina Currie

I did not vote Labour because they've heard of Oasis and nobody is going to vote Tory because William Hague has got a baseball cap.

Ben Elton

Lawless schools produce lawless children.

William Whitelaw

Poverty is considered quaint in the rural areas because it comes thatched.

John Gummer

Europe is my continent, not my country.

John Redwood

When you say you agree to a thing in principle you mean that you have not the slightest intention of carrying it out in practice.

Otto von Bismarck

Actually it's only the urban middle class who worry about the preservation of the countryside, because they don't have to live in it.

Sir Humphrey Appleby

Believe nothing until it has been officially denied.

Claud Cockburn

There is nothing that you could say to me now that I could ever believe.

Gordon Brown to Tony Blair

You might very well think that. I couldn't possibly comment.

Francis Urquhart, the Chief whip in Michael Dobbs's House of Cards

If you don't say anything, you won't be called upon to repeat it.

Calvin Coolidge

Insults

An empty taxi arrived at 10 Downing Street, and when the door was opened, Attlee got out.

Winston Churchill on Clement Attlee

He might as well have a corncob up his arse.

Alan Clark on Douglas Hurd

He has something of the night about him.

Ann Widdecombe on Michael Howard

If I was in the gutter, which I'm not, he'd still be looking up at me from the sewer.

Neil Kinnock on Michael Heseltine

He has sat on the fence so long the iron has entered into his soul.

David Lloyd George on Sir John Simon

When they circumcised Herbert Samuel they threw away the wrong bit.

David Lloyd George

The kind of person who buys his own furniture.

Alan Clark on Michael Heseltine

Mrs Currie loses an enormous number of opportunities to remain silent.

Gerald Kaufman

Peter shook hands with Mickey Mouse and noticed he was wearing a Harriet Harman watch.

William Hague on Peter Mandelson

Peter Mandelson is someone who can skulk in broad daylight.

Simon Hoggart

Like a cushion, he always bore the impression of the last man who sat on him.

Lloyd George on Lord Derby

The difference between a misfortune and a calamity is this: If Gladstone fell into the Thames, it would be a misfortune. But if someone dragged him out again, that would be a calamity.

Benjamin Disraeli

You're an analogue politician in a digital age.

David Cameron to Gordon Brown

Blair goes one way, Brown goes the other way and bang goes the third way.

Michael Howard

I sometimes think that when the prime minister tries to select a weapon it is the boomerang he finds most effective.

John Smith on John Major

Senator, I served with Jack Kennedy. I knew Jack Kennedy. Jack Kennedy was a friend of mine. Senator, you're no Jack Kennedy.

Lloyd Bentsen

With Tony you have to learn to take the smooth with the smooth.

Anonymous senior Labour politician on Tony Blair

He could not see a parapet without ducking beneath it.

Julian Critchley on Michael Heseltine

Michael Heseltine canvassed like a child molester hanging round the lavatories.

Norman Lamont

Savaged by a dead sheep.

Denis Healey's comment on Geoffrey Howe

Compliments

It shows that the substance under test consists of ferrous metal of the highest quality. It is of exceptional tensile strength, resistant to wear and tear, and may be used with advantage for all national purposes.

Enoch Powell on Margaret Thatcher's leadership in the Falklands War

She has the eyes of Caligula and the mouth of Marilyn Monroe.

François Mitterrand on Margaret Thatcher

Others bring me problems. David brings me solutions.

Margaret Thatcher on Lord Young

Backhanded compliments

He's passed from rising hope to elder statesman without any intervening period whatsoever.

Michael Foot on David Steel

A good character is not merely unnecessary for becoming Prime Minister. It may be positively harmful to its owner.

Woodrow Wyatt

Foot in mouth

We'll negotiate a withdrawal from the EEC which has drained our natural resources and destroyed jobs.

Tony Blair, Sedgefield Election Address, 1983

Now is not the time for sound bites. I can feel the hand of history on my shoulder.

Tony Blair, on signing the Anglo Irish Agreement

I am one of a rare breed of true politicians who definitely say what they may or may not mean with absolute certainty.

Sir Anthony Eden

I'm glad I'm not Brezhnev. Being the Russian leader in the Kremlin. You never know if someone's tape recording what you say.

Richard Nixon

It's now a very good day to get out anything we want to bury.

Jo Moore, September 11th 2001

There is a lot of talk about a centre party – and that I might lead it. I find this idea profoundly unattractive.

Roy Jenkins

I don't get a fair whack, I don't pursue vendettas or punch people on the nose.

John Prescott

I have opinions of my own – strong opinions – but I don't always agree with them.

George W. Bush

I'm glad to be back on terra cotta.

John Prescott

Do not underestimate the determination of a quiet man.

Iain Duncan Smith

The quiet man is here to stay and he's turning up the volume.

Iain Duncan Smith

The objectives remain the same and indeed that has been made clear by the Prime Minister in a speech yesterday that the objectives are clear and the one about the removal of the Taliban is not something we have as a clear objective to implement but it is possible a consequence that will flow from the Taliban clearly giving protection to Bin Laden and the UN resolution made it absolutely clear that anyone that finds them in that position declares themselves an enemy and that clearly is a matter for these objectives.

John Prescott

Master of the understatement

I often think how much easier the world would have been to manage if Herr Hitler and Signor Mussolini had been at Oxford.

Lord Halifax

About one fifth of the people are against everything all the time.

Robert F. Kennedy

I think this is the most extraordinary collection of human talent, of human knowledge, that has ever been gathered at the White House – with the possible exception of when Thomas Jefferson dined alone.

John F. Kennedy

The right to be heard does not automatically include the right to be taken seriously.

Hubert Humphrey

I had to prepare the mind of the country and...to educate our Party.

Benjamin Disraeli

The vice-presidency isn't worth a pitcher of warm piss.

John Nance Gardner

I have never made an inflammatory statement in my life.

Reverend Ian Paisley

I fear that within 10 years gays, trade union activists and left wing politicians will be led off to the gas chambers.

Ken Livingstone, 1981

Only a fool wants a confrontation and only a fool wants a strike.

Arthur Scargill, 1977

We know what happens to people who stay in the middle of the road. They get run over.

Aneurin Bevan

The high level of unemployment is evidence of the progress we are making.

Nicholas Ridley

Inflation is as violent as a mugger, as frightening as an armed robber and as deadly as a hit man.

Ronald Reagan

The President has kept all the promises he intended to keep.

George Stephanopolous

A low voter turnout is an indication of fewer people going to the polls.

George W. Bush

It's no exaggeration to say that the undecideds could go one way or another.

George W. Bush

The urgent question of our time is whether we can make change our friend and not our enemy.

Bill Clinton

I can never forgive, but I always forget.

Arthur Balfour

Double entendres

Will this thing jerk me off?

Margaret Thatcher, while firing a field gun during a visit to the Falkland Islands

Every Prime Minister needs a Willie.

Margaret Thatcher on William Whitelaw

Is my right honourable friend saying that Wrens' skirts must be held up until all sailors have been satisfied?

Dame Irene Ward MP on delays in uniforms for the Wrens

How to deploy humour

Paddy Ashdown is the only party leader who's a trained killer. Although, to be fair, Mrs Thatcher was self-taught.

Charles Kennedy

The weak are a long time in politics.

John Gummer

I want to see the hand of history on his collar.

A woman queuing up at the Hutton Inquiry on Tony Blair

Americans have different ways of saying things. They say 'elevator', we say 'lift'. They say 'President', we say 'stupid psychopathic git'.

Alexei Sayle

The main difference for the history of the world if I had been shot rather than Kennedy is that Onassis probably wouldn't have married Mrs Khrushchev.

Nikita Khruschev

How can you govern a country which has 246 varieties of cheese?

Charles de Gaulle

Self deprecation

I have left orders to be awakened at any time in case of national emergency, even if I'm in a cabinet meeting.

Ronald Reagan

A small, balding, ex-communist, Celtic-supporting, Catholic and Unionist. Therefore everyone seems to hate me.

Dr John Reid

Always present, never there.

Denis Thatcher, on being a Prime Ministerial consort

I ask you to judge me by the enemies I have made.

Franklin D. Roosevelt

The main advantage of being famous is that when you bore people at dinner parties they think it is their fault.

Henry Kissinger

I am Al Gore, and I used to be the next President of the United States.

Al Gore

I am extraordinarily patient, provided I get my own way in the end.

Margaret Thatcher

I have been underestimated for decades. I have done very well that way.

Helmut Kohl

I'm used to being unpopular. I'm a Conservative and I'm from Wales.

Nigel Evans

If the fence is strong enough I'll sit on it.

Cyril Smith

I stand astonished at my own moderation.

Lord Clive

I am more or less happy when being praised, not very uncomfortable when being abused, but I have moments of uneasiness when being explained.

Arthur Balfour

I am interested in everything and expert in nothing.

David Amess

Knowing when the end is near

When the final curtain comes down, it's time to get off the stage.

John Major

The first essential for a Prime Minister is to be a good butcher.

William Gladstone

The Prime Minister giveth and the Prime Minister taketh away. Blessed be the name Prime Minister.

Sir Humphrey Appleby

Everyone in active politics has to be conscious of their sell-by date.

Peter Mandelson

It is rather like sending your opening batsmen to the crease, only for them to find that their bats have been broken before the game by the team captain.

Sir Geoffrey Howe, on Mrs Thatcher's style during his resignation speech

Greater love hath no man than this, that he lay down his friends for his life.

Jeremy Thorpe on Harold Macmillan

She was defeated by a collection of 'has beens', 'thought they should have beens', and 'not worth a row of beans'!

Jacques Arnold on Margaret Thatcher's fall from power

My own political future depends upon my own strength of character dealing with the points that are raised.

Charles Clarke

Once I leave, I leave. I am not going to speak to the man on the bridge. I am not going to spit on the deck.

Stanley Baldwin

There's nothing so improves the mood of the party as the imminent execution of a senior colleague.

Alan Clark

There are no true friends in politics. We are all sharks, circling and waiting for traces of blood to appear in the water.

Alan Clark

Former Prime Ministers are like great rafts floating untethered in a harbour.

William Gladstone

I'm a great believer in leaving politics when you've reached your ceiling…Though I did lower the ceiling somewhat.

Cecil Parkinson

A man is not finished when he is defeated. He is finished when he quits.

Richard Nixon

It was like losing my mother. My mother is still alive but one day she won't be, and when that occurs it will, I suspect, be exactly like the day that Margaret Thatcher resigned.

Michael Brown

All political lives end in failure.

Enoch Powell

Sex & morality

I did not have sexual relations with that woman, Miss Lewinsky. I never told anybody to lie, not a single time – never. These allegations are false.

Bill Clinton

Clinton lied. A man might forget where he parks or where he lives, but he never forgets oral sex, no matter how bad it is.

Barbara Bush

Republican boys date Democratic girls. They plan to marry Republican girls, but feel they're entitled to a little fun first.

Anonymous

It's dangerous for politicians to get sucked into private morality and preach to people...Politicians are not saints and I don't pretend to be – and nobody else should pretend to be.

Tony Blair

It always seemed to me a bit pointless to disapprove of homosexuality. It's like disapproving of rain.

Francis Maude

The only safe pleasure for a parliamentarian is a bag of boiled sweets.

Julian Critchley

A hard dog to keep on the porch.

Hillary Clinton on her husband

We must learn to distinguish morality from moralising.

Henry Kissinger

I have never conceived it my duty as a Member of Parliament to seek to amend the Ten Commandments.

Sir John Biggs-Davison

The state has no place in the nation's bedrooms.

Pierre Trudeau

Clinton had sex with loads of women and only had one war. Bush has stuck with his wife and had loads of wars. Draw your own conclusions.

Michael Ehioze Ediae

If I don't have a woman every three days or so I get a terrible headache.

John Fitzgerald Kennedy

They don't call me Tyrannosaurus Sex for nothing.

Edward Kennedy

I've looked on many women with lust. I've committed adultery in my heart many times. God knows I will do this and forgives me.

Jimmy Carter

It depends on what the meaning of the word 'is' is.

Bill Clinton, during his 1998 grand jury testimony on the Monica Lewinsky affair

Index